LEIDOSCOPE

Digestion

Beth Ferguson

Benchmark Books
Marshall Cavendish
99 White Plains Road
Tarrytown, NY 10591
www.marshallcavendish.com

Library of Congress Cataloging-in-Publication Data

Ferguson, Beth, 1968–
  Digestion / Beth Ferguson.
      v. cm. — (Kaleidoscope)
Includes bibliographical references and index.
Contents: You are what you eat — Down the hatch — Mix it up — Small, but important
— The final stop — Excuse me! — When something goes wrong.
  ISBN 0-7614-1591-2
1. Digestive organs—Juvenile literature. [1. Digestive system.] I.
Title. II. Series: Kaleidoscope (Tarrytown, N.Y.)
QP145.F47 2003   612.3—dc21   2003000662

Photo research by Anne Burns Images

Cover photo: Custom Medical Stock Photo

The photographs in this book are used with the permission and through the courtesy of:
Photo Researchers Inc./Science Photo Library: 36; Professor Peter Cull, 7; CNRI, 15; Scott Camazine/Science Source,
20; John Bavosi, 23; David Gifford, 24; Bob Shepherd, 27. *Custom Medical Stock Photo:* 8, 12, 32. *Cajun Images:* Kate
White, 11. *Phototake:* 16, 19. *Superstock:* 31, 40, 43. *Corbis:* Tom Stewart, title page; Gaetano, 4; ROB&SAS
Photography, 28; Ronnie Kaufman, 35; Larry Williams, 39

Series design by Adam Mietlowski

Printed in Italy

6 5 4 3 2 1

Contents

You Are What You Eat

Your body does many things all by itself. You don't have to think about breathing. You never have to make sure your heart is beating or wonder whether your hair is growing. All these things happen on their own—as long as you give your body the **nutrients** it needs.

Nutrients come from the foods you eat. Meat and eggs are full of **proteins** and **fats**. Bread and pasta are good sources of **carbohydrates**. Fruits and vegetables have plenty of **vitamins** and **minerals**. Your body needs all these nutrients to stay healthy.

◄ *Did you eat a sandwich for lunch? It will help give your body the nutrients it needs.*

Your **digestive system** breaks down these foods and releases their nutrients. Then your blood carries the nutrients to all the cells in your body, so you can walk and talk, read and write, swim and sleep, think and grow. During your lifetime, more than 50 tons of food may pass through your digestive system.

Two views of the stomach: the drawing on the left shows the folded surface of the stomach lining. The many powerful muscles that aid digestion are shown on the right. ▶

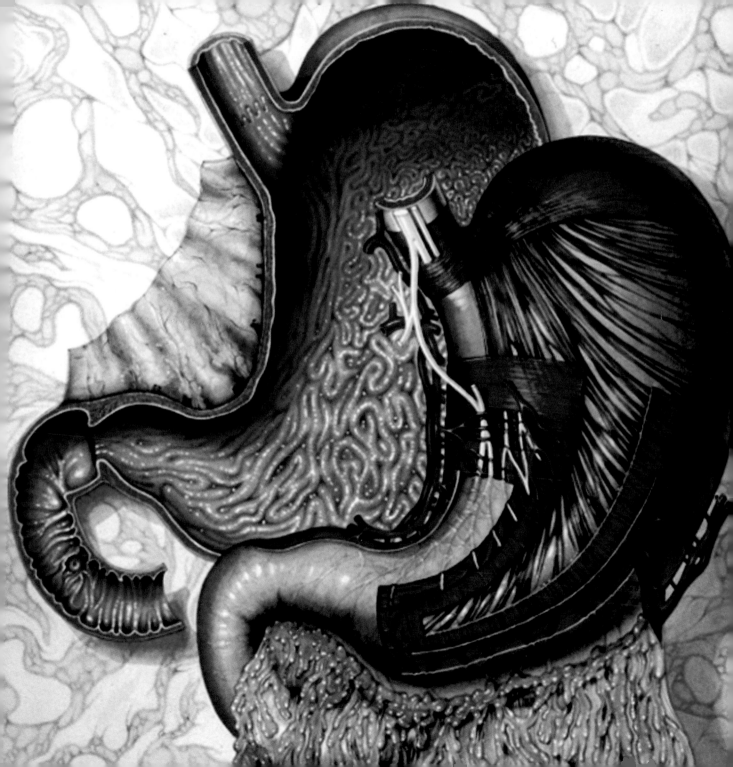

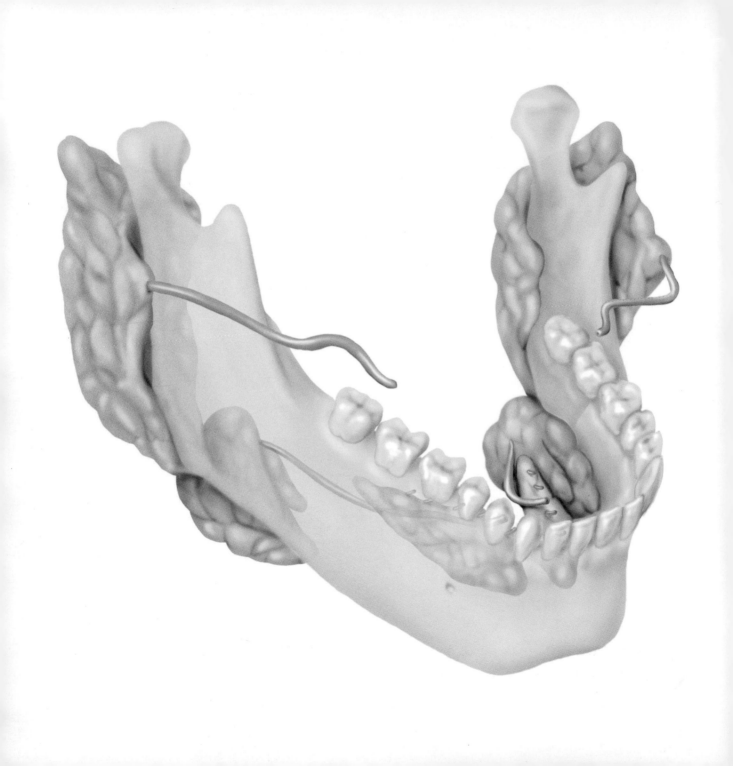

Down the Hatch

Digestion begins the moment you take a bite of food. Most of the time, you chew food for five to thirty seconds. As your teeth cut and grind, **glands** in your cheeks and under your tongue add **saliva**. Chemicals in your saliva begin to break down **starch**—a kind of carbohydrate found in plants. Your body makes about 1 quart (1 liter) of saliva every day.

◀ *This drawing shows the lower jaw, the glands that make saliva, and the tubes that carry saliva to the mouth.*

As you are chewing, your tongue rolls the mashed food into a soft, moist ball and pushes it to the back of your throat. When you swallow, a flap called the **epiglottis** closes off your **trachea**, or windpipe, so food doesn't get into your lungs. But if you talk while you are eating, your epiglottis may not close. If this happens, you can choke.

As soon as you swallow, rings of muscle surrounding your **esophagus** push food toward your **stomach** in the same way that you squeeze toothpaste out of a tube. When food reaches the bottom of the esophagus, a valve opens and food passes into your stomach. Then the valve quickly closes, so food cannot move back into your esophagus.

Digestion starts in your mouth. Your tongue shapes the food into a ball ▶
as saliva starts to break it down.

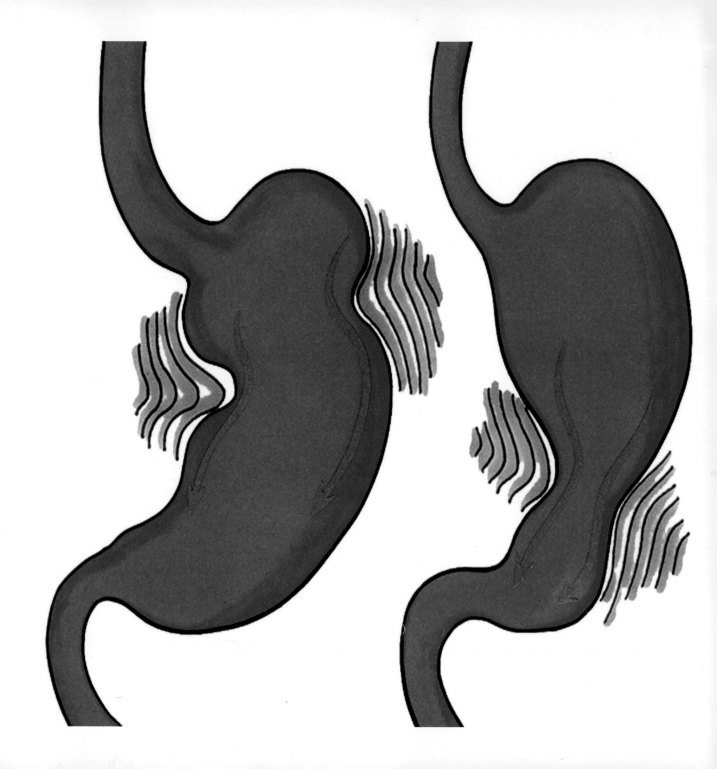

Mix It Up

Your stomach is a pouch that can stretch like a balloon to hold more and more food. When it is full, the stomach's strong, muscular walls begin to squeeze, mix, and churn the food. These muscles **contract** about three times a minute.

Thousands of tiny glands line the inside of your stomach. They make about 2 quarts (2 liters) of digestive juices every day. As the juices mix with your food, they soften it and kill any germs you have swallowed.

◀ *Your stomach contracts, or squeezes together, to mix the food you eat.*

A few hours after you have eaten, your meal has become a thick, soupy mixture called **chyme**. By this time, some simple carbohydrates have been completely digested and have passed into your bloodstream. Proteins and fats have begun to break down.

Muscles move the chyme forward until it reaches another valve. Each time the valve opens, a little bit of the chyme is pushed into the **small intestine**. All this happens inside your body without you thinking about it.

This photograph of the lining of a stomach was taken through a high-power microscope. Around the larger cells are droplets of mucus, colored yellow here, which help protect the stomach. ▶

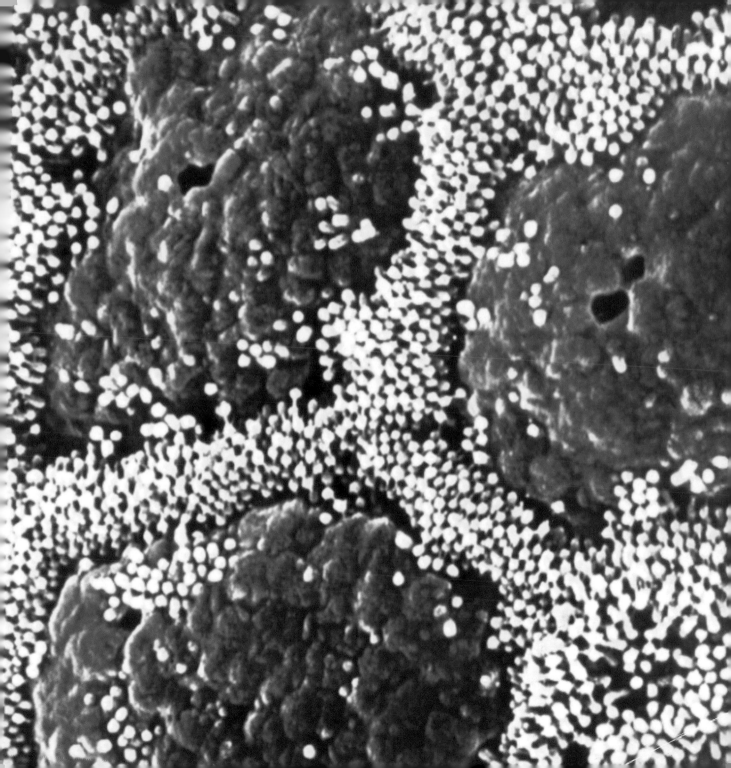

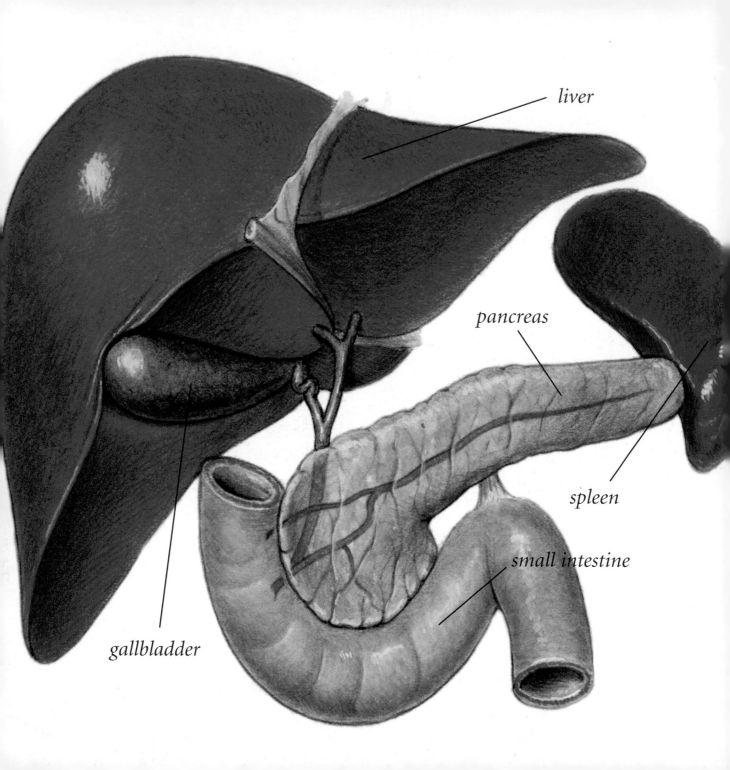

liver

pancreas

spleen

small intestine

gallbladder

Small But Important

Your small intestine is a narrow, twisting tube coiled up inside your body. It is about 1 inch (2.5 centimeters) wide, but more than 20 feet (6 meters) long. Soon after food enters your small intestine, more digestive juices pour in from the **pancreas** and **gallbladder**. Other digestive fluids flow out of glands in the walls of the small intestine.

The pancreas and the liver each make about 1 quart (1 liter) of digestive juices every day. The juices from the pancreas break down complex carbohydrates, proteins, and some fats. The juices from the gallbladder are called bile. Bile is made in the **liver**, but stored in the gallbladder between meals. It is especially good at breaking down fats.

◀ *This drawing shows how the liver, gallbladder, pancreas, and small intestine are arranged in the body. Digestive juices from the liver, gallbladder, and pancreas help you break down food.*

After the bits of food in chyme have been completely digested, the nutrients enter your bloodstream. They are absorbed through the walls of the small intestine. These walls are not smooth like the sides of a garden hose. They are covered with millions of tiny, fingerlike structures called **villi**. Each of these villi is lined with even smaller **microvilli**. Villi and microvilli increase the total surface area of the intestinal walls by about 150 times. This makes it easier for nutrients to pass through the walls and enter the tiny **blood vessels** that surround the small intestine.

Once the nutrients have entered the blood, they travel to cells all over the body. You use some of the energy from carbohydrates right away. The leftover energy is stored so you can use it later.

This photograph, which was taken through a high-power microscope, shows some of the tiny microvilli that line the surface of the small intestine.

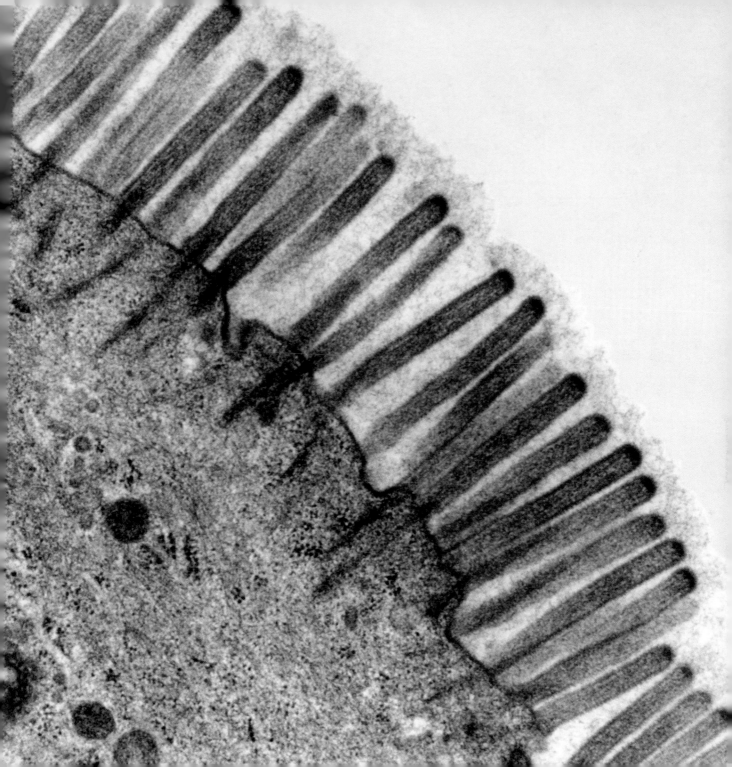

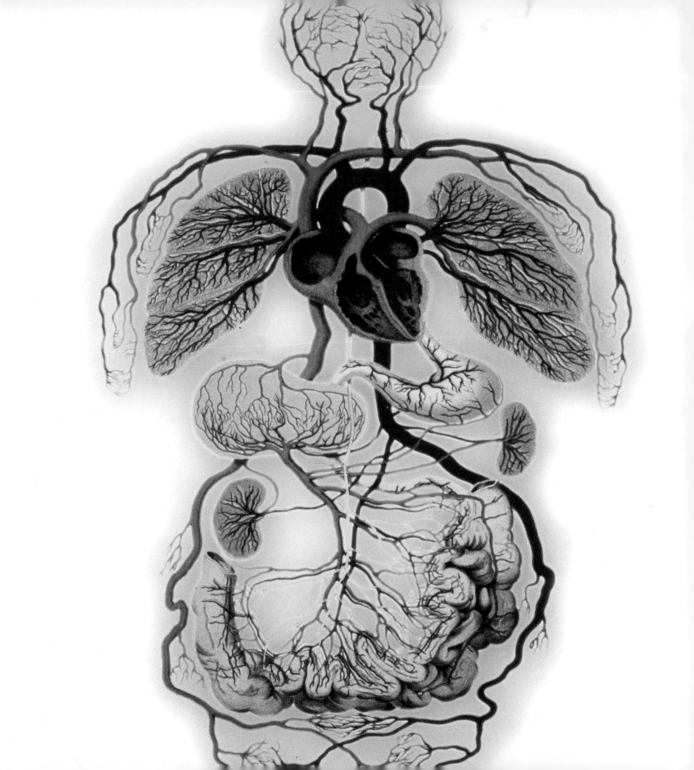

The proteins from your food have been broken into smaller materials called **amino acids**. Your body puts the amino acids back together to create new proteins. Some of these proteins speed up chemical reactions in your body. Others are used to repair damaged cells and build new bones, hair, muscles, and skin as you grow.

Like carbohydrates, fats give you energy. They also protect your inner organs, help keep you warm on cold days, and build the nerves that carry messages to and from your brain.

Vitamins are important because they help turn fats and carbohydrates into energy. They also protect you from diseases and help build bones and blood cells. Like vitamins, minerals help your body build bones and blood cells. They also keep your teeth strong and make sure there is always enough water in your body.

◀ *Your bloodstream is like a system of highways. It moves nutrients to all parts of your body.*

The Final Stop

After spending up to six hours in the small intestine, undigested material moves into your **large intestine**—an upside-down U-shaped tube that wraps around the small intestine. It is 5 to 6 feet (1.5 to 2 m) long and about 2.5 inches (6 cm) wide.

Even though the large intestine is much shorter than the small intestine, material may spend more than eighteen hours there. During that time, muscles surrounding the large intestine press against the material inside. Most of the water is squeezed out of the chyme. The large intestine absorbs about 1.5 gallons (6 l) of water every day. This water is then reused by the body. The large intestine also collects salt. Bacteria living inside the large intestine make vitamin K, which helps to stop the bleeding when you cut yourself.

In this drawing, you can see the inside and the outside of the large intestine. ▶

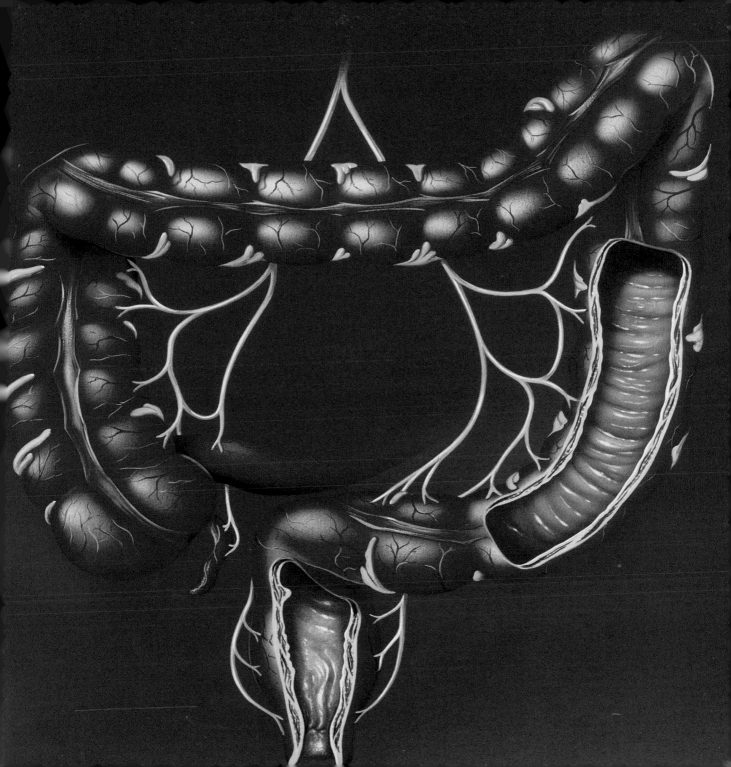

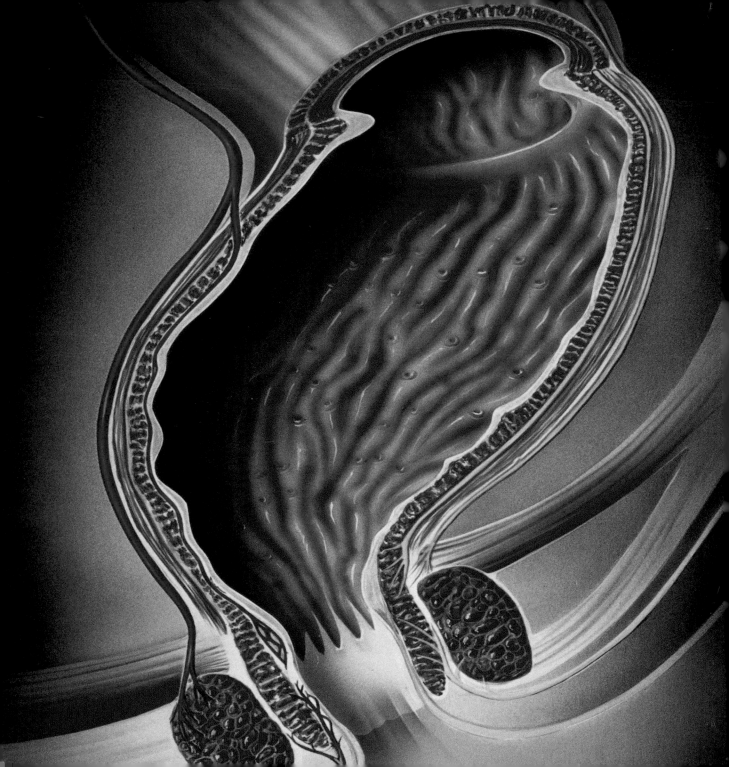

As the large intestine absorbs water, the chyme becomes drier and harder. At this point, the waste material contains food bits that could not be digested, digestive juices, dead bacteria, old cells from the lining of the digestive system, and a small amount of water. All these materials are pressed into a brown mass called **feces**. The feces are then stored in your **rectum**. When you go to the bathroom, a valve at the end of your rectum opens, and feces are released through your **anus**.

◀ *Feces are stored in the rectum and pass out of the body through the anus, the opening shown at the bottom of the drawing.*

Another common problem is the hiccups. You can get the hiccups if you eat too much food or if you eat when you are excited or upset. When you have the hiccups, your diaphragm—the large muscle above your stomach—suddenly tightens. As you breathe, your diaphragm normally moves up and down in a steady rhythm. But if your stomach expands too much, this gentle movement may be disrupted. This can force extra air into your lungs and cause your vocal cords to suddenly snap. When you try to breathe out, the air hits your vocal cords, making an unexpected "hic" sound.

◄ *How do you cure the hiccups? Some people think having a friend jump out and scare you when you are not expecting it is the best way.*

When you eat foods with a lot of **fiber**, you may have a different problem. Fiber is the tough, outer covering of plants. Beans, bran, broccoli, cabbage, oatmeal, prunes, and radishes are all good sources of fiber. Your body cannot digest fiber, so it passes quickly through your small intestine. When it reaches your large intestine, bacteria living there start to break it down. As the bacteria feed on the fiber, they produce a gas that gradually builds up in your large intestine. When the pressure becomes too great, the valve at the end of your rectum opens and some of the gas passes out of your body. Sometimes the gas moves so quickly it makes a popping noise.

Cabbage is one food that is rich in fiber.　▶

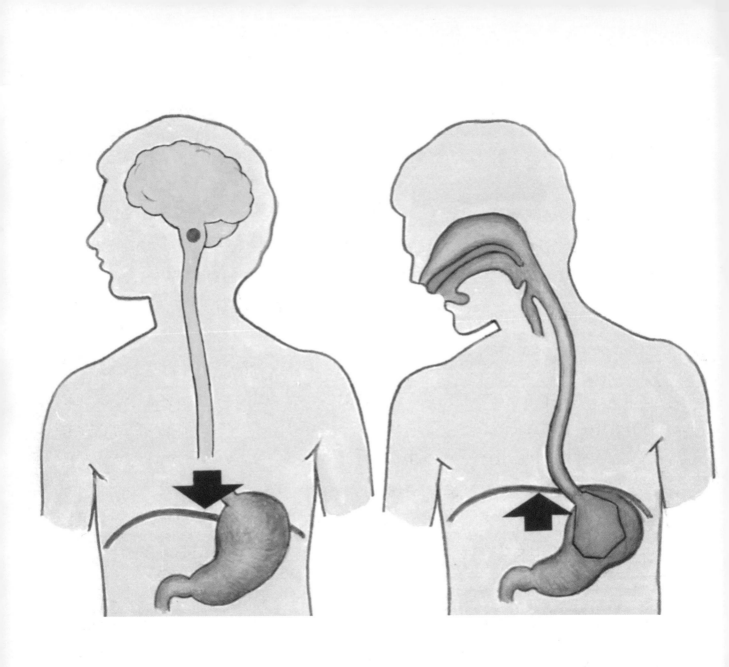

When Something Goes Wrong

Your digestive system usually has no trouble doing its job, but there may have been times when your stomach hurt. Maybe you even threw up or had **diarrhea**. These problems are usually caused by germs in the foods you eat. Most germs are destroyed by the digestive juices in your stomach, but some manage to survive. They can cause stomach flu or traveler's diarrhea.

Throwing up is your body's way of getting rid of harmful materials in your stomach. Diarrhea helps rid your body of harmful materials in your intestines. When you have diarrhea, your feces are loose and watery because the water has not been squeezed out yet. Most of the time, it doesn't take very long to get the harmful materials out of your digestive system. Once they are gone, you usually start to feel better.

◀ *Normally food travels down the esophagus and into your stomach. But when you've eaten something harmful, the body may get rid of it, sending the food in the opposite direction.*

Diarrhea is bad, but **constipation** can feel much worse. When a person is constipated, his or her large intestine absorbs too much water. This may happen if material is moving through the large intestine too slowly. The waste material gets so hard and dry that the muscles around a person's rectum have trouble pushing it out of the body. If you feel constipated, one of the best things you can do is eat foods high in fiber. Because fiber passes through your digestive system quickly, it can help move out other materials too. Drinking lots of water also helps move food along.

Most stomachaches are caused be germs in the foods you eat. ▶

If you feel a steady, throbbing pain near your right hip, you may have an infection called **appendicitis**. Your **appendix** is a small, worm-shaped structure attached to your large intestine. Long ago, it may have helped with digestion, but now it is useless. Sometimes the appendix becomes infected. If an infected appendix is not removed, it may burst and spread the infection.

◀ *The appendix is a slim, finger-shaped tube (left) attached to the large intestine.*

Some people get sick when they eat certain foods. Do you get a rash when you eat chocolate? Do your eyelids or lips swell when you eat nuts? You may have a food **allergy**. An allergy occurs when your **immune system** attacks a material that is not normally harmful to people. Anyone can get allergies, but they are more common in children than in adults. Some scientists think that children are more likely to develop a food allergy if they are given a food too early in life. Eggs, pork, seafood, nuts, wheat, milk, bananas, oranges, and strawberries are just some of the foods that can cause allergies. If you are allergic to a certain kind of food, you will have to eat other foods that have the same nutrients.

For some people, chocolate is one treat that can cause a bad reaction. ▶
Even the smallest amount can cause problems.

A Healthy Digestive System

To keep your digestive system working smoothly, you should eat plenty of fiber. Each day, choose foods that are rich in carbohydrates, vitamins, and minerals. Eat moderate amounts of meat and other foods that are high in protein. Most importantly, try to avoid candy, cookies, and other foods that contain a lot of sugar and fat.

◄ *Fruits and vegetables are good sources of vitamins and minerals.*

Before a snack or meal, take a few minutes to wash your hands. When you help your parents cook, think about ways to keep harmful bacteria out of your food. Do not thaw frozen foods on the counter, and always cook meat thoroughly. If you remember these simple rules, your digestive system will have no trouble doing its job.

When you are cooking, make sure your hands are clean and try to keep ▶
harmful bacteria out of your food.

Glossary

allergy—A medical condition in which your immune system attacks a material that is not normally harmful to people.

amino acid—One of the building blocks of proteins.

anus—The opening through which feces pass out of the body.

appendicitis—A medical condition that develops when the appendix becomes infected.

appendix—A useless structure attached to the large intestine.

blood vessel—One of the tubes that carries blood throughout the body.

carbohydrate—A nutrient that provides the body with energy.

chyme—A thick, soupy mix of partially digested food and digestive juices.

constipation—Unable to move feces out of the body.

contract—To shorten; to push or squeeze together.

diarrhea—Very watery feces.

digestive system—The parts of the body involved in breaking down food and absorbing nutrients.

epiglottis—A flap that closes during swallowing, so food will not enter the lungs.

esophagus—The tube that connects the mouth and the stomach.

fat—A nutrient that stores energy in the body.

feces—The solid waste material that leaves the digestive system.

fiber—The tough outer covering of many plants.

gallbladder—A body organ that stores bile, a kind of digestive juice.

gland—A small structure that makes and releases digestive juices.

immune system—The parts of the body involved in attacking germs.

large intestine—The part of the digestive system that absorbs water. It also contains bacteria that make vitamin K and feed on fiber.

liver—A body organ that makes bile.

microvilli—Tiny structures that form on villi and help nutrients move from the small intestines into the blood.

mineral—A nutrient that helps build bones and blood cells, keep teeth strong, and make sure there is always enough water inside your body.

nutrient—A substance that keeps the body healthy.

pancreas—A body organ that makes digestive juices.

protein—A nutrient made of amino acids. Proteins speed up chemical reactions, repair damaged cells, and build new bones, hair, muscles, and skin as you grow.

rectum—The section of the large intestine that temporarily stores feces.

saliva—Spit, digestive juices made by glands in the mouth.

small intestine—The part of the digestive system that breaks down food particles and allows nutrients to pass into blood vessels.

starch—A kind of carbohydrate that is partially broken down in the mouth.

stomach—The part of the digestive system where simple carbohydrates are absorbed and digestion of complex carbohydrates, fats, and proteins begins.

trachea—The tube that connects the mouth and the lungs.

villi— Tiny structures that form on the walls of the small intestine and help nutrients move into the blood.

vitamin—A nutrient that helps turn other nutrients into energy, provide protection from diseases, and build bones and blood cells.

Index